# KINGDOM CLASSIFICATION

## PROTOZOANS, ALGAE & OTHER
# PROTISTS

By Steve Parker

*First published in the United States in 2009 by*
Compass Point Books
151 Good Counsel Drive
P.O. Box 669
Mankato, MN 56002-0669

KINGDOM CLASSIFICATION—PROTISTS
was produced by:

**David West Children's Books**
7 Princeton Court
55 Felsham Road
London SW15 1AZ

 This book was manufactured with paper containing
at least 10 percent post-consumer waste.

*Designer:* Rob Shone
*Editors:* Gail Bushnell, Anthony Wacholtz
*Page Production:* Bobbie Nuytten

*Creative Director:* Joe Ewest
*Art Director:* LuAnn Ascheman-Adams
*Editorial Director:* Nick Healy
*Managing Editor:* Catherine Neitge

**Library of Congress Cataloging-in-Publication Data**
Parker, Steve, 1952–
 Protozoans, algae & other protists / by: Steve Parker.
  p. cm.—(Kingdom classifications)
 Includes index.
 ISBN 978-0-7565-4224-5 (library binding)
 1. Protista—Juvenile literature. 2. Protozoa—Juvenile
literature. 3. Algae—Juvenile literature.
I. Title. II. Title: Protozoans, algae and other protists.
III. Series: Parker, Steve, 1952– Kingdom classifications.
 QR74.5.P37 2009
 579—dc22      2009008783

Visit Compass Point Books on the Internet at
*www.compasspointbooks.com*
or e-mail your request to
*custserv@compasspointbooks.com*

PHOTO CREDITS :
Abbreviations: t-top, m-middle, b-bottom, r-right,
l-left, c-center.

3, NOAA/David Burdic; 6–7, 14br, 20–21, 22, 27b, Roland
Birke; 6b, Captain Albert E. Theberge, NOAA Corps (ret.);
8tr, ARS/USDA/Eric Erbe; 8tl, 8mr, Environmental Protection
Agency; 8ml, 43bl, Image by Ute Frevert, false color by
Margaret Shear; 9ml, 39bl, Jason Hollinger; 9br, 16t, 18t,
Eric Grave; 10tr, 12r, Dr. Ralf Wagner; 11ml, 42b, CDC/ Dr.
George Healy; 12t, 21b, 26, 28–29, 39t, 39br, Carolina
Biological Supply Company; 12br, Scott Fay, UC Berkeley,
2005; 13b, 14l, 23b, Oxford Scientific; 14tr, Jean Schweitzer;
15br, OSF/James Dennis; 16–17, 17br, 19b, 27tr, 29b, 32,
38l, Dennis Kunkel; 19l, Richard Kirby; 19r, Felix Andrews;
20, 25l, Aurora Nedelcu; 23r, Bruno de Giusti; 24b, David
M. Dennis; 25t, Laguna Design; 28tl, Ben Blankenburg; 28bl,
Gunter Küchler; 30t, Paul Erickson; 30bl, 30bc, 30br, NOAA
Image courtesy of H. Scott Meister, SCDNR; 30mr, Norvin
Knight; 31l, Heather Craig; 31tr, Heiko Hübscher; 31bc, TH
Foto-Werbung; 32bl, John Wigham; 32br, Eric Moody; 33,
NURC/UNCW and NOAA/FGBNMS; 34l, Vera Bogaerts;
34br, NASA; 34r, Kristen Johansen; 35br, Kheng Guan Toh;
36t, 36r, 36bl, Don Barr; 37tl, Gnangarra; 37cr, D. Inglis;
37b, Devon Stephens; 41t, Andrew David, NOAA/NMFS/
SEFSC Panama City/Lance Horn, UNCW/NURC–Phantom II
ROV operator; 41b, Yuuji Tsukii, Protist Information Server;
42cr, 43br, CDC/Dr. Edwin P. Ewing, Jr.; 42ml, CDC; 43tm,
CDC/ Dr. Francis W. Chandler; 43tr, CDC/ Donated by the
World Health Organization (WHO), Geneva, Switzerland;
43mr, CDC/ Dr. D.S. Martin; 43bml, CDC/Jim Gathany.

Every effort has been made to contact copyright
holders of any material reproduced in this book.
Any omissions will be rectified in subsequent
printings if notice is given to the publishers.

*Front cover: Slime Mold*
*Opposite: Green algae*

# KINGDOM CLASSIFICATION

# PROTOZOANS, ALGAE & OTHER
# PROTISTS

*Steve Parker*

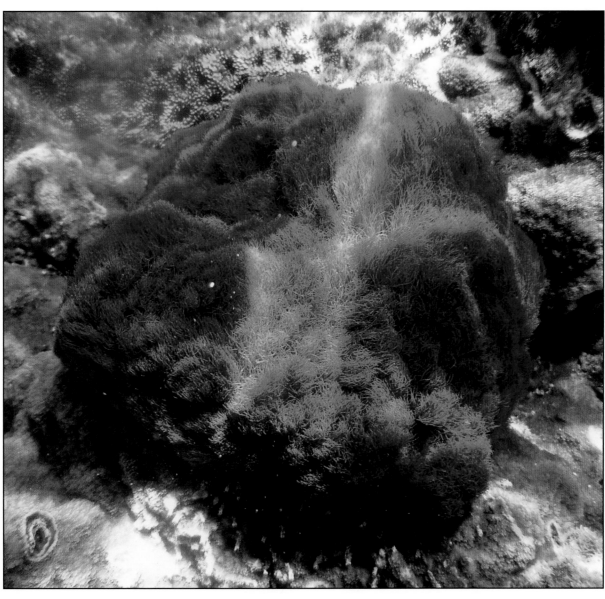

Compass Point Books ◆ Minneapolis, Minnesota

# TABLE OF CONTENTS

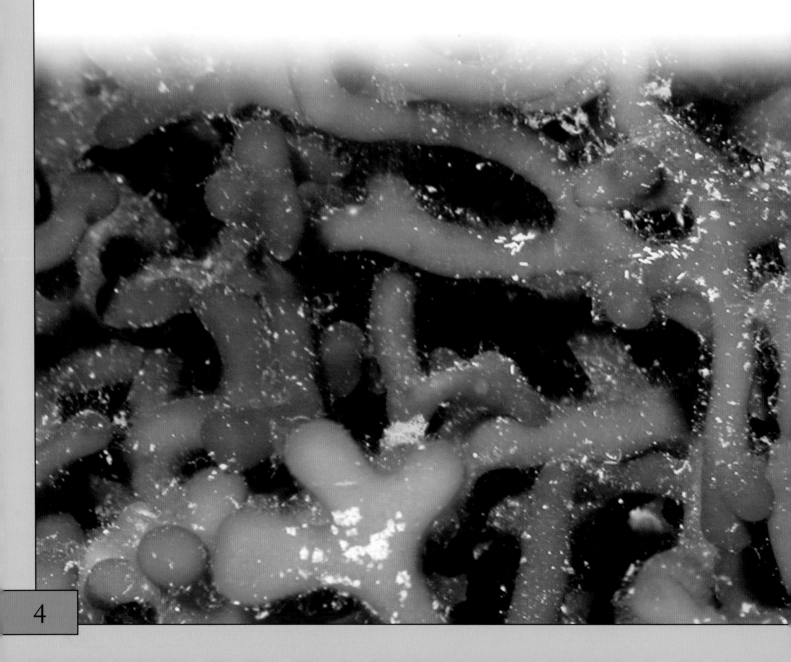

# INTRODUCTION

Although protists are almost everywhere you look, you cannot see them. They are mostly microscopic life-forms, each made of one living unit called a cell. Some protists are like tiny animals because they take in or eat food. They are often called protozoans. Other protists, the protophytans, are like tiny plants because they use the sun's light energy to grow. Some protists have traits of both plants and animals.

There are thousands of kinds of protists. The tiniest are so small that a thousand would fit into this "o." Others, such as algae, can grow bigger than a person.

*ALGAE (SEAWEED)*
*The biggest protists look like plants and grow in salty water. Some experts group them in the kingdom Plantae with other plants, such as mosses, ferns, flowers, and trees. But inside their bodies, algae are much simpler than true plants.*

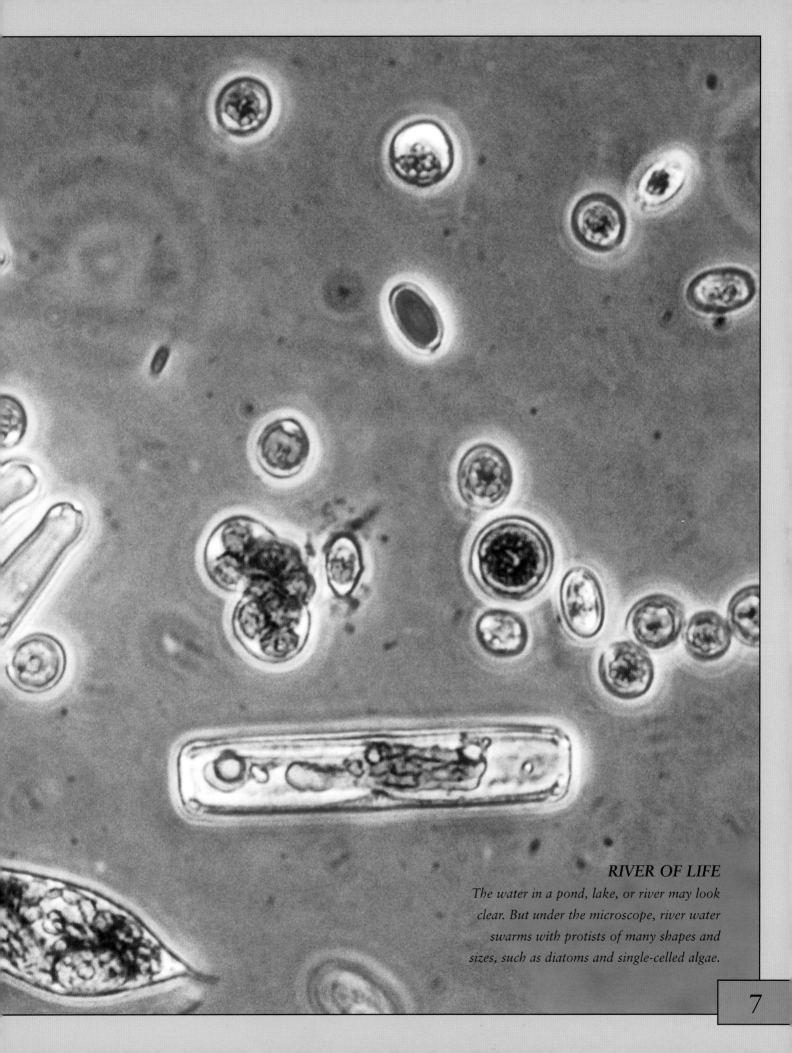

**RIVER OF LIFE**
The water in a pond, lake, or river may look
clear. But under the microscope, river water
swarms with protists of many shapes and
sizes, such as diatoms and single-celled algae.

# WHAT ARE PROTISTS?

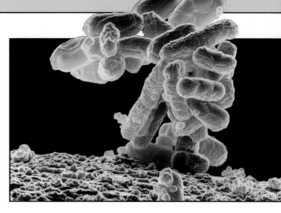

**P**rotists are such a varied group that when describing what they are, it helps to first explain what they are not.

**NOT PROTISTS**
Microbes called bacteria are a single cell each. But their lack of inner membranes means they are not protists.

## PROTISTS ARE NOT ...

The living world is divided into groups known as kingdoms. Three of the main kingdoms are animals, plants, and fungi. Organisms in these three kingdoms have more than one microscopic cell. They usually consist of millions of cells of various kinds.

Most protists are made up of only one cell. If they have lots of cells, most of the cells are of the same kind. Protists live almost everywhere—in water and soil, on rocks, and on (and in) other living things.

**LIFE IN WATER**
Most protists live in freshwater or sea-water. Microscopic diatoms (above) can be found in the Great Lakes.

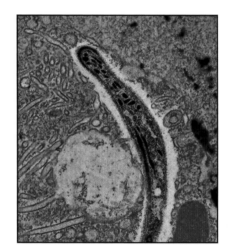

**KILLER PROTISTS**
Several deadly diseases around the world are due to infection by protists, such as Plasmodium, *which causes malaria.*

**SHAPELY PROTISTS**
*Diatoms are plantlike protists with shapes such as rods, balls, boxes, and stars.*

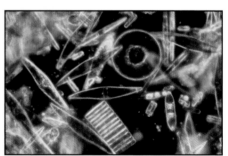

**HELPFUL PROTISTS**
*Corals are colonies of simple animals. Inside their bodies are millions of protists called zooxanthellae, which help the corals obtain nutrients.*

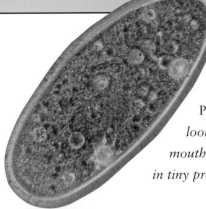

## PREDATORY PROTISTS

Paramecium *is a furry-looking protist with a mouthlike opening that takes in tiny prey such as bacteria.*

### WEEDY PROTISTS

*Algae come in many shapes and colors, including red, green, and brown.*

## IMPORTANCE OF MEMBRANES

There are two basic kinds of cells. The prokaryotic cell has an outer layer—a cell membrane—but no separate membranes inside. The eukaryotic cell has membranes inside, enclosing substances such as the cell's genetic material, DNA. Protists are eukaryotes. Living things such as bacteria are prokaryotes. They are even smaller and simpler than protists.

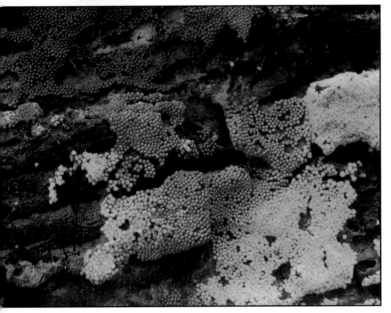

### SLIMY PROTISTS

*On land, most protists thrive in damp conditions, such as in soil, under stones, and on tree trunks and rotting logs.*

## DISCOVERING THE "ANIMALCULES"

*Dutch cloth merchant van Leeuwenhoek (1632–1723) made microscopes that magnified 300 times.*

By 1595 the first microscopes allowed people to see the tiniest living things for the first time. Pioneer microscopist Anton van Leeuwenhoek was amazed by the wriggling things he saw, calling them animalcules.

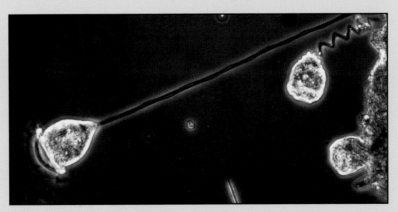

*In 1702 van Leeuwenhoek was the first person to see and describe* Vorticella, *a cup-shaped protist with a long stalk.*

# PARTS OF A PROTIST

**M**ost protists may be small, but this does not make them simple. They have many parts.

**LIVING BLOB**
*Amoebas are common bloblike protists usually found in water, mud, soil, and other damp places.*

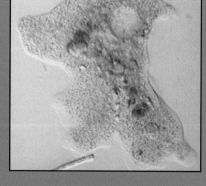

Outer membrane

Folds (cristae)

Matrix

**MITOCHONDRIA**
*Sausage-shaped mitochondria are energy centers. They provide energy from food for life processes such as growth and movement.*

## ORGANELLES

Animals have main parts inside called organs, each with an important task. For example, the heart pumps blood. A protist like an amoeba (below) has parts inside, too, known as organelles. Each organelle plays a vital role in keeping the whole protist alive.

Uroid

Food vacuole

Oil crystal

Water vacuole

## VACUOLES
*Substances such as water, food, and wastes are wrapped up inside the protist in baglike parts called vacuoles. The water vacuole contains spare water that the protist may need if conditions dry out.*

Nucleolus

Genetic material

Pore

Nuclear membrane

## NUCLEUS
*The nucleus is the protist's control center. It contains deoxyribonucleic acid, or DNA, that holds the instructions for how the protist grows and survives.*

## AMOEBOID MOVEMENT

Amoeba protists are soft and squishy, like a plastic bag filled with water. They change shape by pulling or pushing various parts of the cell membrane.

An amoeba can flow along like a slug. It can also send out "arms" called pseudopods. To move, it flows the rest of its main fluid body, the cytoplasm, into the arms.

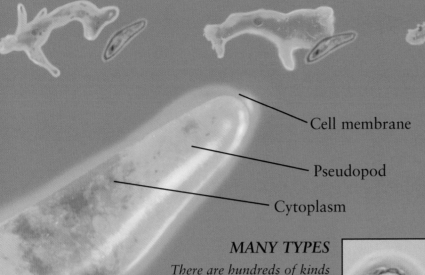

Cell membrane

Pseudopod

Cytoplasm

### MANY TYPES

*There are hundreds of kinds of amoebas. Some can cause illnesses in people, such as redness at the front of the eye (keratitis), swelling of the brain (encephalitis), and digestive infection (dysentery).*

### HOW SMALL ARE PROTISTS?

Most protists are about 1/2500 to 1/50 of an inch (0.01 to 0.5 millimeters) across. The smallest are about the same size as the red cells in your blood—and there are 5 million of those in one pinhead-sized drop.

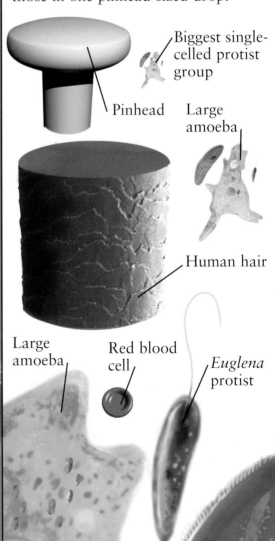

Biggest single-celled protist group

Pinhead

Large amoeba

Human hair

Large amoeba

Red blood cell

*Euglena* protist

### FEEDING

*An amoeba is a protozoan. It consumes food, but it does not have a mouth. It eats by extending pseudopods (meaning "false feet") around its victim to surround it and take it in.*

*Paramecium* being eaten

# HUNGRY PROTISTS

**P**rotists are small. But the animal-like ones, protozoans, hunt even tinier living things. They take in tiny bits of food.

### THE SOIL JUNGLE
Soil is home to many animals, from moles to insects and worms. Look much closer and there is a micro-jungle of protists, bacteria, and similar living things hunting each other. Various kinds of amoebas ooze between soil particles as they engulf smaller protists and bacteria. The *Gymnophrys* amoeba extends its tentacles into long, thin spikes that feel for pieces of food.

*BACTERIA-EATER*

*The amoeba* Euglypha *lives in a protective casing called a test.*

*FEEDING FRENZY*

Chaos *is a giant amoeba as big as the dot on this "i."
A* Chaos *(above) feeds on many* Paramecium *protists (green blobs).*

### WATER HUNTERS
Most kinds of protists live in water, where they are not in danger of drying out and can move about by floating. Some kinds have long thin parts called feeding processes sticking out from the main cell body. These catch anything edible floating past. Such protists include foraminiferans in the sea. They have bendable, netlike feeding processes sticking out of a test, its central shell, made of chalk minerals.

*DRIFT NETS*

*Foraminiferans have long thin strands of cytoplasm that trap food particles drifting past.*

## THE "BRAIN-EATING" AMOEBA

The protist *Naegleria fowleri* usually lives in warm freshwater, such as tropical rivers and lakes. However, it may change into an amoeba-like shape and infect the human body through the nose. It multiplies in the brain and nervous system and causes so much damage that it is often fatal.

*Water-skiers can be at risk of getting protist infections.*

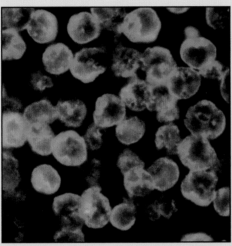

Naegleria fowleri *can survive harsh conditions in the form of a cyst with a thick, tough case.*

## SURROUNDED BY SPIKES

Radiolarians are protists that live in the sea. Each has a complicated double shell made of plates of hard silica (the same mineral as in grains of sand). Radiolarians divide the main cell body into outer and inner compartments. They also have stiff, spikelike projections called axopods that help them to float. Heliozoans are similar but without the central double shell.

### MICRO-SUNS

*The axopods of a heliozoan, or "sun animal," stick out in all directions like the rays of the sun.*

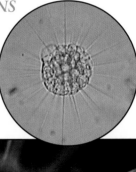

### STARS

*After radiolarians die, their empty shells sink to the bottom and form seabed mud called radiolarian ooze.*

# LIGHT-LOVING PROTISTS

**P**lantlike protists capture the sun's light energy to make energy-rich substances, which they use as food to grow and survive.

*GREEN WATER*
*In warm, sunny conditions, plantlike protists can grow and multiply so fast that they turn the water a cloudy green color.*

## POWERED BY THE SUN

The process of trapping light energy to make food is known as photosynthesis. All plants do it, which means they are autotrophs, or "self-feeders."

Many kinds of protists are autotrophs, too. They carry out photosynthesis using carbon dioxide gas from the air and water. These are joined using light energy to make energy-containing substances, such as sugars. The protist can then break apart the sugars and release the energy to power its life processes, such as growth and getting rid of waste. Photosynthesis also produces oxygen, which humans and animals must breathe to stay alive.

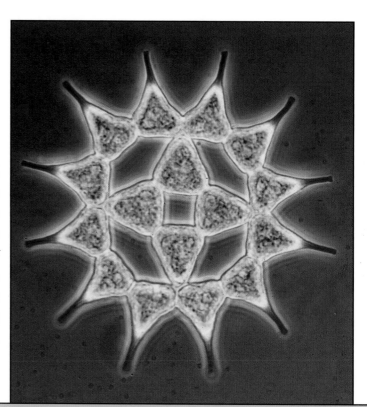

*GREEN STAR*
*Pediastrum is a colonial green algae, meaning it lives as a group of cells. Some are on the inside, and others are around the outside, forming a starlike shape.*

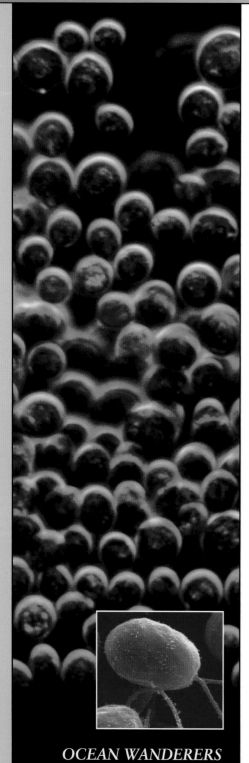

### OCEAN WANDERERS
*Among the most common plantlike protists are the green algae called Chlamydomonas. Each has a long whiplike "tail" for swimming (inset).*

## OCEAN FOOD CHAINS

Plants grow using light energy. Herbivorous animals eat the plants, and carnivore animals eat other creatures. In this way, food chains exist in nature.

Land plants are mostly easy to see, such as grasses, flowers, and trees. Their place is taken by trillions of plantlike protists, especially algae. These are food for animal-like protists, which are eaten by slightly bigger creatures, such as baby fish and crabs, and so on along food chains to huge fish and whales.

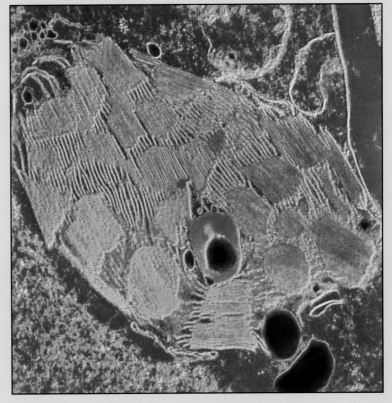

### PLANKTON

*Plantlike protists such as dinoflagellates (inset) make up plankton. This feeds slightly bigger organisms and eventually large creatures such as whale sharks.*

## CHLOROPLASTS

Inside many plantlike protists are organelles called chloroplasts. They look like stacks of sheets or plates. This is where the protist captures light energy and turns it into food. Long ago, chloroplasts may have had free-living bacteria called blue-green algae that got into a larger cell and made a home there. They provided the bigger cell with food, In return they had somewhere safe to live. This type of relationship where both partners benefit is called symbiosis.

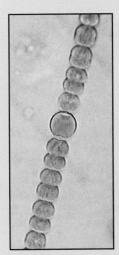

*Bacteria known as blue-green algae may have become chloroplasts.*

*The layers of a chloroplast are known as thylakoids.*

15

# SURVIVAL SPECIALISTS

One of the best-known protists is *Euglena*. It can use light energy like plants or take in nutrients from its surroundings.

## ON THE PROWL

Most kinds of *Euglena* are so small that 500 of them in a row would stretch just 1 inch (2.5 centimeters). They live in freshwater ponds, rivers, and lakes, while a few kinds live in salty water.

Usually *Euglena* captures light energy from the sun by photosynthesis, using parts inside called chloroplasts. Some *Euglena* also have a "mouth" at the front to eat prey, such as bacteria. Others take in nutrients through their surface from the water around them.

### GREEN SWARMS

*When spring brings more sunlight and warmth, Euglena multiplies rapidly in ponds and puddles. Its increasing numbers give the water a greenish color.*

Paramylon granules
(stored food reserves)

Mitochondria

Tail end

Cytoplasm (inner fluid)

### CHLOROPLASTS

*These contain a green substance known as chlorophyll that traps light energy from the sun. If Euglena stays in the dark, its chloroplasts shrink and the protist turns pale. The chloroplasts regrow when it comes back into the light.*

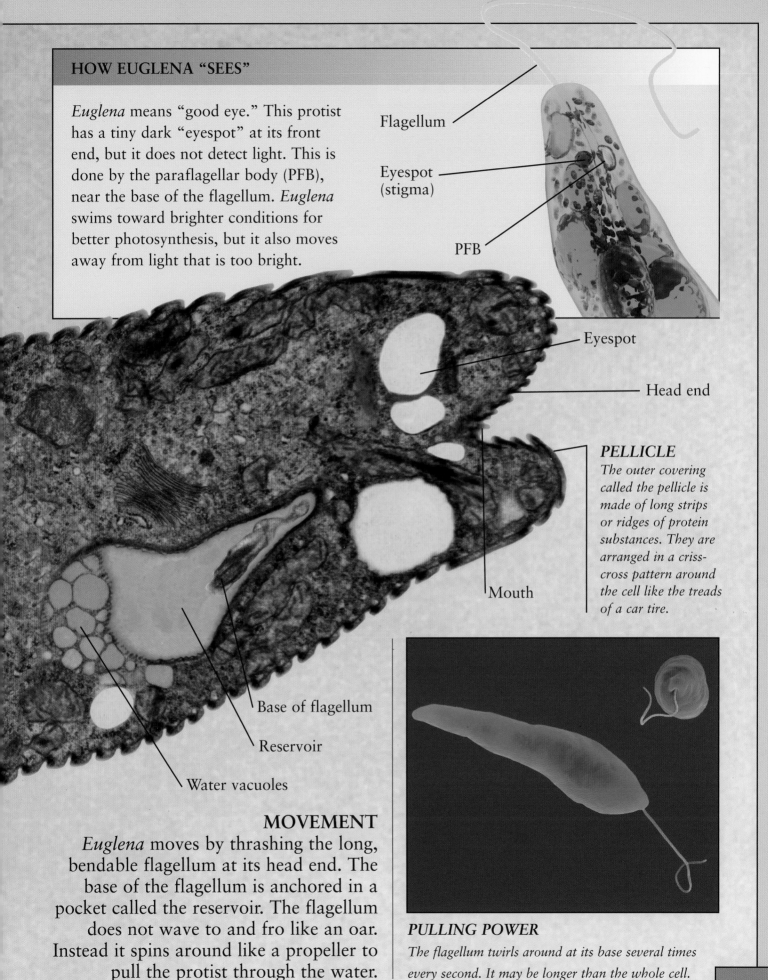

## HOW EUGLENA "SEES"

*Euglena* means "good eye." This protist has a tiny dark "eyespot" at its front end, but it does not detect light. This is done by the paraflagellar body (PFB), near the base of the flagellum. *Euglena* swims toward brighter conditions for better photosynthesis, but it also moves away from light that is too bright.

Flagellum

Eyespot
(stigma)

PFB

Eyespot

Head end

### PELLICLE
*The outer covering called the pellicle is made of long strips or ridges of protein substances. They are arranged in a criss-cross pattern around the cell like the treads of a car tire.*

Mouth

Base of flagellum

Reservoir

Water vacuoles

## MOVEMENT
*Euglena* moves by thrashing the long, bendable flagellum at its head end. The base of the flagellum is anchored in a pocket called the reservoir. The flagellum does not wave to and fro like an oar. Instead it spins around like a propeller to pull the protist through the water.

### PULLING POWER
*The flagellum twirls around at its base several times every second. It may be longer than the whole cell.*

# HAIRY PROTISTS

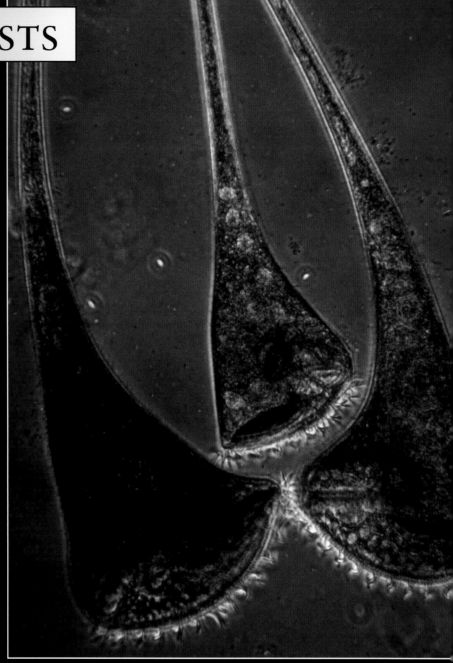

**U**nder a high-power microscope, some protists seem to have a fuzzy or furry coat. These are the ciliates, with tiny hairs called cilia.

## MANY USES

Cilia are common in the living world. We have them lining the airways in our lungs and other internal parts. Ciliate protists have them on the outside, either all over or only in certain places. The cilia are usually arranged in rows, zigzag lines, or similar patterns. They wave back and forth like sets of microscopic oars or a big crowd doing a stadium wave. This helps the protist move by swimming or crawling. It also creates water currents to bring in floating food, to help the protist attach to an object, or to allow it to detect nearby movements.

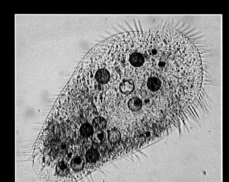

### DUAL CONTROL
*Freshwater* Tetrahymena *is widely used in science research, partly because it has two nuclei, one large (blue) and the other small.*

### GIANT WITH A "CROWN"
Stentor *is a massive protist, up to ¼ inch (6 mm) in length. In ponds and rivers, it attaches to weeds or rocks and sweeps in tiny food with its crownlike circle of cilia.*

### ALL OVER
*Under a microscope, cilia at the visible edge of a protist can be seen clearly. The rest of the cilia are not visible.*

Among the most common protists in nature, as well as in classrooms and scientific studies, are *Paramecia*. Some kinds grow to the size of the period at the end of this sentence. *Paramecia* live mainly in fresh water. The cilia coating them help them to swim with a spinning motion, either backward or forward, depending on which way they wave. An oral groove has cilia to sweep food particles into the protist's mouth.

*Millions of* Paramecium *live in scummy water where they consume algal protists.*

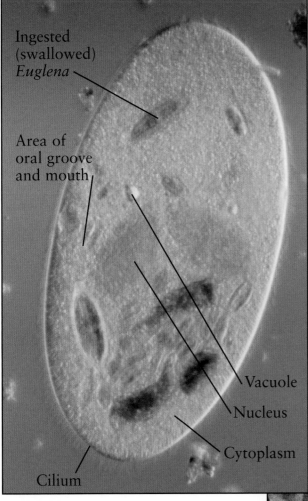

Ingested (swallowed) *Euglena*

Area of oral groove and mouth

Vacuole

Nucleus

Cytoplasm

Cilium

Paramecium *draws in and "swallows" tiny prey, such as bacteria, other protists, and microscopic fungi, such as yeast cells.*

*A close-up of* Paramecium *cilia (each with a brown outline) shows how they fit close together like fibers in a carpet. A basal body (blue) fixes each cilium into the cell membrane. The shaft of the cilia contains sets of protein called microtubules (dark green stripes) that help with movement.*

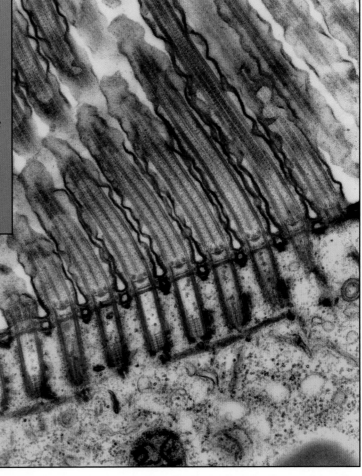

# LIVING TOGETHER

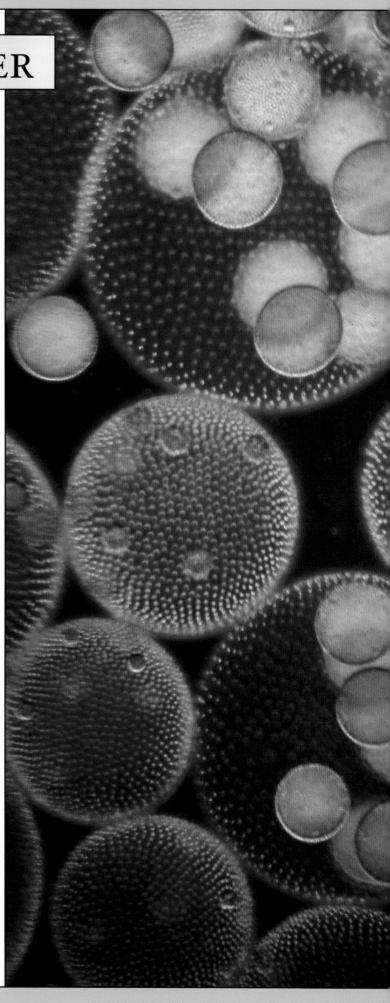

**P**rotists that live together with others of their kind are known as colonial. Sometimes there are just a few protists. In other colonies, there may be thousands.

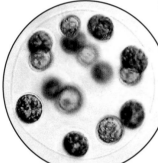

## SMALL BALLS

*The green algal protist* Eudorina *forms ball-shaped colonies with 32 cells in each.*

### COMMUNAL LIFE

Some colonial protists form random clumps with no special organization or pattern. In other types, the colonies are neatly arranged in rows, circles, or balls.

Usually the individual protists making up the colony are all the same. They are not specialized into various types of cells, as are the cells in an animal or plant. The protist colony members gain protection from being surrounded by others. They can also share food. The whole colony is too big to be eaten by the tiny creatures that normally hunt single protists.

### BIG BALLS

*Green* Volvox *forms large, ball-shaped colonies with several thousand members. They grow best in warm, nutrient-rich freshwater, creating a green haze. Some of the colonies are as large as the dot on this "i."*

## PROTIST, PLANT, ANIMAL?

In some colonial protists, the individual member cells have slight differences. For example, in a large *Volvox* ball, some cells on one side have better developed eyespots to detect light. As they do this, all the cells beat their flagella in a coordinated way to swim toward the light, like a tiny animal. This means they can carry out photosynthesis more effectively, like a tiny plant. So *Volvox* is midway between a colony of separate protists and a single multicelled living thing—a combination of plant and animal.

*SPOTTY SCUM*
*Colonial green protists can grow so fast that their tiny groups merge to form green floating scum.*

### GREEN SLIMY HAIR

*Spirogyra* is a green algal protist that lives as long chains of cells called filaments, similar to beads on a necklace. The filaments form slimy hairlike growths in ponds and rivers and are eaten by water creatures such as tadpoles and pond snails. *Spirogyra's* chloroplasts are arranged in a spiral-like pattern called a helix (like a corkscrew).

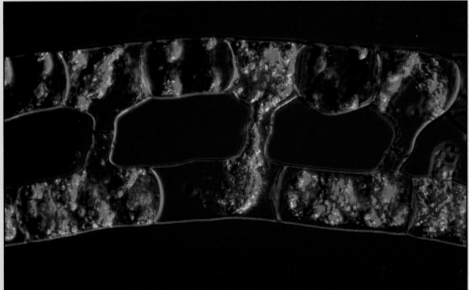

*The green filaments of* Spirogyra *can grow side branches to each other as a form of reproduction.*

# PROTISTS WITH WHIPS

The dinoflagellates are protists with flagella—long, whip-like tails that they use to move around. Most kinds live in water.

## VARIOUS SHAPES

Dinoflagellates have many shapes, such as boxes, golf balls, and pyramids with long spiky horns. Many types have an outer protective covering of scalelike plates called the theca. Most have two flagella. One flagellum wraps around the cell and waves to make the protist move along and turn around. The other flagellum is at one end and controls the direction.

## VITAL LINKS

Some dinoflagellates are like plants, growing by photosynthesis. Others are micro-hunters, taking in smaller living things as prey, including other dinoflagellates. In the sea, these protists form a vital part of the "living soup" of plankton, which is food for slightly larger creatures. Some types can even glow in the dark, which is called bioluminescence.

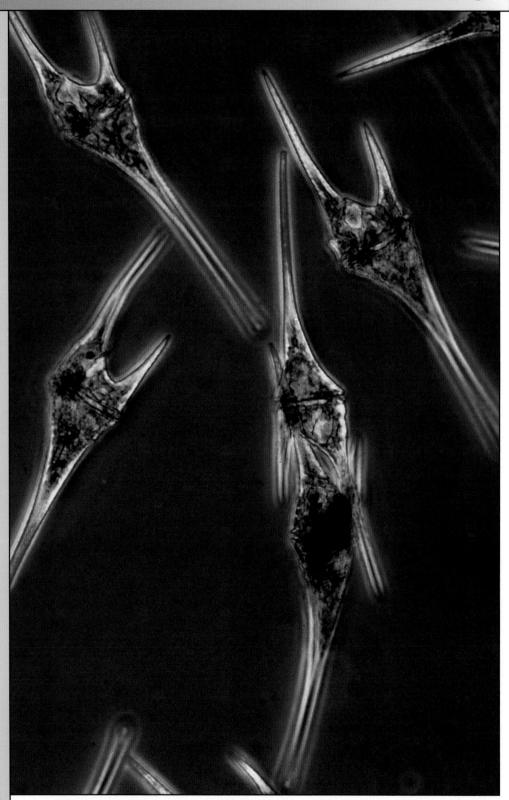

*POINTY HORNS*

Ceratium *is a common dinoflagellate with long horns. It lives in the upper layers of seas and lakes, where there is enough light for photosynthesis.*

In calm waters with plenty of warmth and nutrients, algal protists can sometimes multiply out of control. This is known as an algal bloom. Their bodies turn the water strange colors, and their waste products collect and make it poisonous to fish and other creatures.

*A toxic red tide stains the water and endangers animal life.*

## GOOD RELATIONS

Some dinoflagellates live inside the bodies of coral polyps, which are animals. They carry out photosynthesis and share their food with the coral, which gives them a place to live in return—an example of symbiosis.

### SUNLIT CORALS

*Coral animals live in warm, shallow water (inset). They catch tiny prey with their stinging tentacles. They also rely on dinoflagellate protists, known as zooxanthellae, which look like green dots in the coral's tentacles (below). So corals can only flourish in water that gets plenty of sunlight.*

# PROTIST LIFE CYCLES

**P**rotists have many ways of growing and making more of their kind. Sometimes they join to breed, like animals. At other times, one protist simply splits into two.

## FAST AND SIMPLE
When a protist divides into two, a process known as binary fission, the "offspring" have the same genes as the original parent. They are clones of the parent—they look the same and live in exactly the same way. This type of reproduction is fast and simple. It works well if conditions remain constant. But if conditions change, the protists are unable to adapt to them because their genes cannot alter.

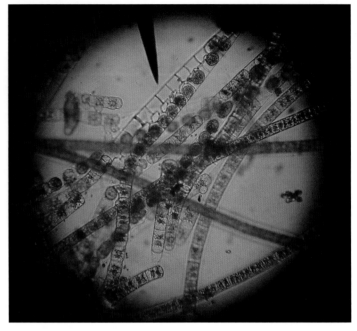

*GENE TRANSFER*
*Algal protists may start conjugation when there is a sudden change in their surroundings, such as a rapid fall in temperature or a new kind of nutrient available.*

## CONJUGATION
Another form of reproduction in protists happens when individuals transfer DNA with each other. Known as conjugation, this may bring together new combinations and versions of genes in the offspring, which allow them to survive in new and changing conditions.

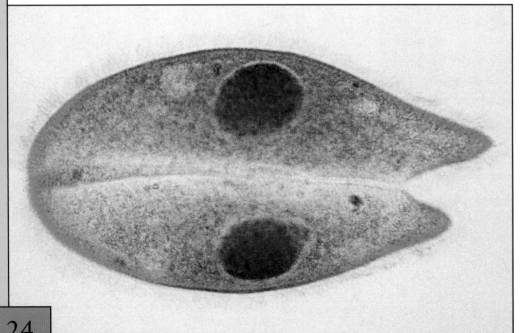

*PROTIST MATING*
*Two Paramecia conjugate by exchanging genetic material from their nuclei (red spots).*

## BINARY FISSION

*A ciliate protist splits into two daughter cells. Some ciliates are unusual in having a large nucleus, a macronucleus, or perhaps even two or more. They might also have several smaller ones known as micronuclei. All of these make duplicates of their DNA before they divide. This ensures that each daughter cell receives a full set of DNA, called the genome.*

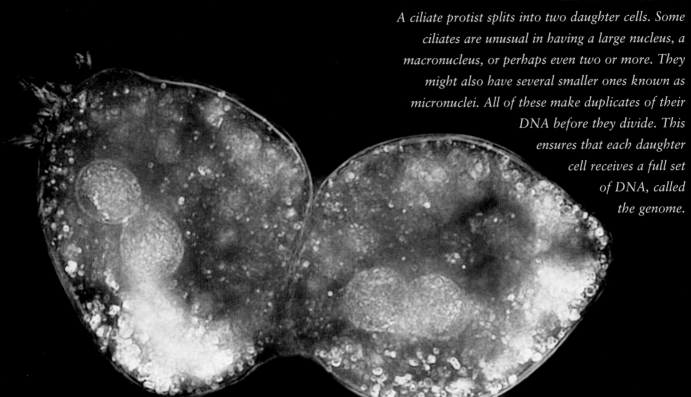

## VERSATILE VOLVOX

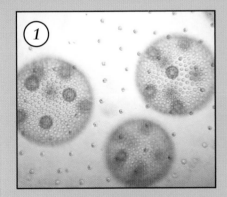

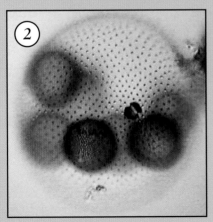

*Volvox* colonies have several ways of breeding. In asexual reproduction, part of a colony may break off and grow into a new, full-sized one. Or new daughter colonies may grow inside an existing one (1, green balls inside the larger colonies). The daughter colonies then break out. In sexual reproduction, the colonies produce sperm called micro-gametes (1, floating dots outside the colonies) and large eggs called oogametes. A sperm joins an egg, and the resulting zygote multiplies by binary fission to form a new full-sized colony (2).

## BREEDING PROTISTS

Many protists also breed by sexual reproduction. Instead of transferring genetic material, they make tiny parts called gametes (sex cells) that contain genetic material. Two gametes join and combine their genes to form an offspring, called a zygote, with a new combination of genes. The zygote may form a thick-walled cyst around itself for protection. Under good conditions, the zygote enlarges into a full-grown adult.

# THE TINIEST ALGAE

Diatoms are among the most numerous living things in the world. They form up to half of all the algae (plantlike protists) in seas, oceans, and freshwater.

## GLASS HOUSES

There are probably more than 100,000 species of diatoms. Their amazing shapes vary from spheres, rods, and triangles to boxes, wheels, vases, and stars. Each diatom is a single cell and makes its own protective shell, called a test or frustule. This consists of two halves known as valves. One valve is slightly smaller than the other and fits into it around the edges.

### JEWELS OF THE SEA

*Diatoms sparkle because their cases are made of silica—the same mineral we use to make glass. The clear case lets in light so the diatom can trap its energy by photosynthesis.*

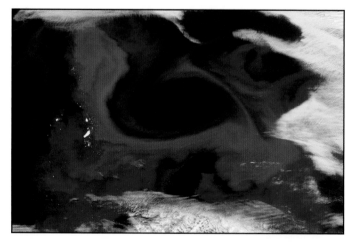

### DIATOM BLOOM

*As with other kinds of plantlike protists, diatoms can multiply quickly in conditions of bright light, warmth, and plentiful nutrients. They cause a bloom that colors the water, but they soon use up all the nutrients and die.*

The tests of diatoms are hard enough to be preserved as microfossils in rocks. Some of these fossils are more

*Diatoms thrived in prehistoric seas.*

than 200 million years old, from before the dinosaurs. The various diatom types from different times in the past show whether the seas were warm or cold, shallow or deep, and clear or cloudy. This allows scientists to build a picture of how the oceans have changed through the ages.

*A pinpoint-sized diatom fossil magnified*

## USEFUL INDICATORS

Certain diatoms prefer certain water conditions. So the types that grow in a particular place indicate the quality of water there. They are called indicator species. For example, some cannot live in even tiny amounts of pollution.

### TAKING SAMPLES

*Diatoms are useful as indicators to show whether water is clean or polluted. Tabellaria (below) is common in large lakes. However, if the water is polluted, some diatoms do not grow as well. Scientists take water samples and study them under the microscope to see which kinds of diatoms are most common to measure water quality.*

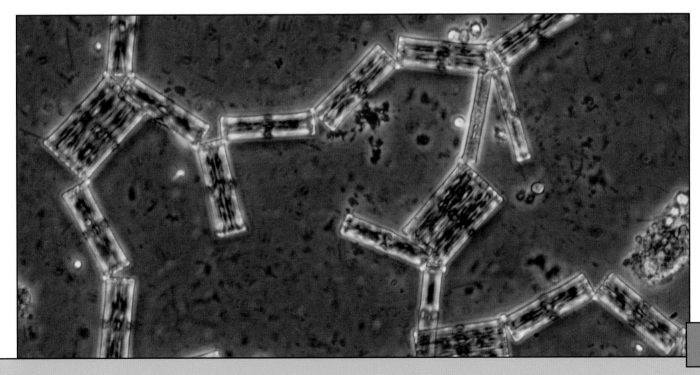

# GOLDEN ALGAE

**N**ot all protists that trap sunlight by photosynthesis are green. Chrysophytes are known as golden algae because of their beautiful colors.

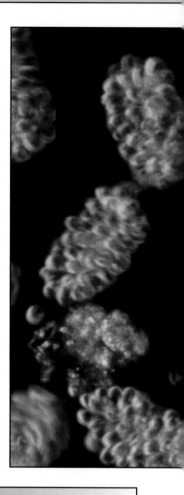

### GOLDEN WATER
*Huge numbers of golden algae can give lake water a yellowish-green or olive-green tinge.*

### COLORFUL
Green algae and green plants get their color from chlorophyll. This colored substance, called a pigment, soaks up the energy in sunlight for photo-synthesis. But green is not the only photosynthetic color. Some algae are various shades of gold, yellow, amber, or brown because they have different photosynthetic pigments, such as xanthophyll and fucoxanthin.

### FRESHWATER
Many golden algae live in freshwater lakes, where they form the basis of many food chains. Some are free-floating single cells. Others form colonies shaped like balls, ribbons, or hair.

### AT HOME IN THE MANGROVES

The golden algae *Vaucheria* does not dry out because it has rootlike parts called siphons that grow into wet mud or sand. These algae thrive in marshes and other freshwater wetlands. They also grow along coasts, such as in mangrove swamps, where they are exposed to air as the tide goes out.

### GOLDEN ALGAE
*There are more than 1,000 species of golden algae. Some grow in fuzzy, hairy patches.*

*Golden algae make mangrove mud firm.*

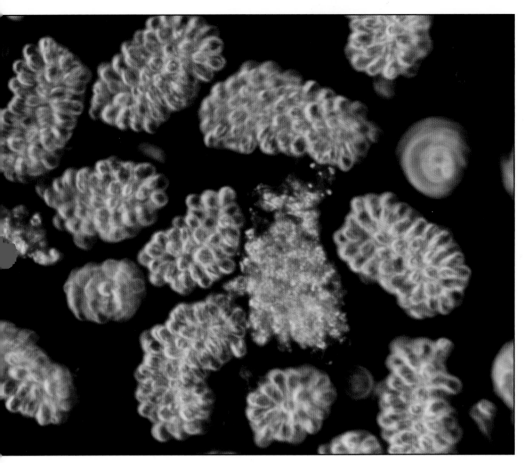

## SWITCHING OVER

Some golden algae look like amoebas. Others are covered in tiny scales made of silica and similar minerals.

Not all species of golden algae carry out photosynthesis all the time. Some can switch from trapping the sun's light energy to absorbing nutrients from the water directly through their outer surface. This is useful when light levels are low, such as in the winter or during cloudy weather. If nutrients are scarce, some golden algae even become predators. They eat diatoms, bacteria, and other tiny prey.

*SWIMMING CLUSTERS*

*Synura is a scaled algae whose individual protist cells are covered in silica plates. It forms clusterlike colonies that swim by moving their flagella.*

*STARTLING SHAPES*

*Asterionella (above) is named after its starburst shape and can grow as big as this "o." Mallomonas (right) has a long body covered with overlapping scales like a pine cone.*

# BROWN ALGAE

The biggest protists by far are the phaeophytes, or brown algae. They include brown seaweed, such as wracks, oarweeds, and rockweeds.

### TRUE GIANT

*The giant kelp* Macrocystis *can grow to more than 165 feet (50 meters) in length—the size of a big tree—in a single year.*

## TOUGH LIVING

There are more than 1,500 species of brown algae around the world. Most live along rocky seashores. They are leathery and tough, able to cope with stormy weather, crashing waves, and rolling boulders. Some have air-filled bladders that help them float at the surface, where there is the most light for photosynthesis.

### BROWN RAFT

*Sargassum and other brown algae of the Sargasso Sea form a dense, tangled mat that floats like a raft. It is home to strange fish, crabs, and other creatures.*

## THE FLOATING SEA

The Sargasso Sea in the western Atlantic Ocean is a vast tropical area of floating sargassum weed and other brown algae. It forms an unusual habitat for creatures found nowhere else.

### WASHED UP

*Storms can tear brown seaweed from rocks and wash them onto the beach.*

### SARGASSO CREATURES

*The frogfish (1) uses its front fins to crawl among sargassum weed. The scrawled filefish (2) is one of the largest Sargasso creatures. The porcupine fish (3) has long spines for protection.*

## SLEEPING IN A KELP BED

Huge underwater beds of giant kelp are home to many specialized kinds of fish, shellfish, prawns, and other creatures. Sea otters live in the kelp beds along the west coast of North America. The smallest ocean-living mammals, otters wrap themselves in floating kelp fronds to feed and sleep.

*Sea otters rest and feed in kelp beds, safe from big waves.*

*HOLDING FAST*

*Brown algae have fasteners, called holdfasts, that attach to rocks. But the holdfast does not take in water or nutrients like a true plant's roots.*

## PLANTS OR NOT?

Some brown algae look quite complicated on the outside. They have bodies with various parts, such as a holdfast (root), a stipe (stem), a thallus (main body), and fronds (leaves). But their inside parts do not have as many specialized kinds of cells as the roots, stems, and leaves of true plants.

Some experts group the brown algae with true plants rather than with the protists. Others put them in another main group, the heterokonts. This is because of the detailed structure of their chloroplasts.

*USEFUL CURE*

*Brown wracks (above left) and other algal seaweed are rich in the mineral iodine. They are collected and dried (above) to obtain iodine, which is used to treat goiter, a disease in people. A lack of iodine in the body can cause the thyroid gland in the neck to swell (right).*

# RED ALGAE

**R**ed seaweed, also known as rhodophytes, are the largest group of algae with up to 10,000 species worldwide.

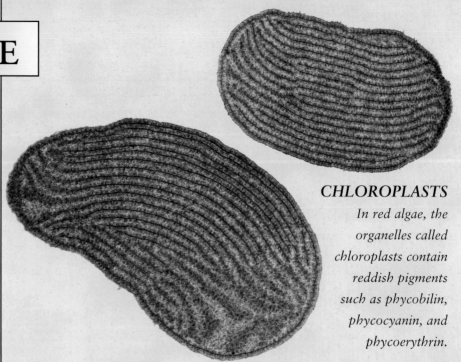

## CHLOROPLASTS
*In red algae, the organelles called chloroplasts contain reddish pigments such as phycobilin, phycocyanin, and phycoerythrin.*

## RED OVER GREEN
Red algae get their colors from the pink, red, or mauve pigments that soak up light energy to carry out photosynthesis. Water absorbs different colors of light with increasing depth. Red pigments work better than green ones in the deeper waters where red algae usually live.

## HANDY ALGAE
The red algae *Chondrus crispus*, also known as carrageen or Irish moss, is used in many experiments. It is a good model for investigating photosynthesis and similar processes.

### SCIENTIFIC SEAWEED
*Carrageen is a common algae used in many scientific studies.*

## USEFUL RED SEAWEEDS

*Red seaweeds like laver and dulse are used in cooking.*

Several kinds of red algae are collected and used by people. Carrageen, dulse, and laver contain many healthy minerals and other substances. They are eaten in various forms, such as raw with vegetables or salads, or boiled into a pulp. Laver can be baked with oatmeal into laver bread.

*Irish moss is named for its thin strands that resemble true moss.*

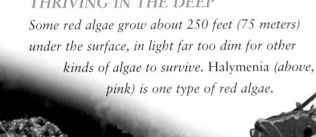

## CORALLINE

Red algae are among the oldest groups of living things, other than microscopic life-forms. Their fossils date back more than 500 million years. Then, as now, they helped to build coral reefs. Coralline red algae such as *Corallina*, *Spongites*, and *Lithophyllum* are stiffened with calcium or chalk minerals. They form hard mats that grow with the stony, cuplike cases of coral animals. These form reef rocks with cracks, crevices, and caves where fish and other creatures hide.

**THRIVING IN THE DEEP**

*Some red algae grow about 250 feet (75 meters) under the surface, in light far too dim for other kinds of algae to survive. Halymenia (above, pink) is one type of red algae.*

**RHODOLITHS**

*Some coralline red algae grow in clumps that tumble along the sea bed, pushed by water currents. As they become weighed down with their chalk minerals, they settle and spread out in hard lumpy layers known as rhodoliths.*

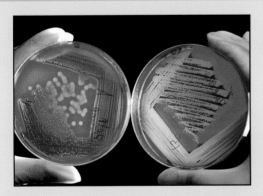

*Microbes such as bacteria and protists are grown in the laboratory on jellylike substances known as agars. These are made from red algae and other seaweeds.*

*A plate of dulse*

Red algae, such as dulse, are rich in jellylike starchy substances called carrageenans. These are purified and used in many ways, such as for thickeners to make sauces, desserts, and ice cream less runny. They are also used in products such as toothpaste, paper, shoe polish, and fire-fighting foam.

*Red seaweed extracts make ice cream smoother and thicker.*

# MAKING MORE ALGAE

Algae such as seaweeds look simple in structure, with few of the specialized parts found in true plants. But the ways many of them breed are more complicated.

## BROKEN BITS

Some algae multiply when they are broken into pieces, such as by strong waves. The separate parts grow into new organisms. This is known as asexual, or vegetative, reproduction. The new algae are clones and have the same genes as their parent.

### SEAWEED FARMS
*Knowing how seaweed reproduce helps farmers get the conditions right so the algae breed well.*

## TWO-STAGE LIFE

*In brown algae such as kelp, the main seaweed is known as the sporophyte stage. It makes tiny zoospores that can swim. These grow into small, separate male and female plants that produce gametes, or sex cells. A sperm and egg join and grow back into the main sporophyte plant.*

## DIATOMS

Diatoms can split themselves in two by binary fission. Usually each valve grows a new, smaller partner. The shell size gets smaller with each new generation. Once they reach a minimum size, they form a stage called an auxo-spore. Then they reproduce sexually with eggs and sperm to form full-sized diatoms again.

### READY TO BREED
*Diatoms multiply quickly in warm water with plenty of sunlight.*

## MANY STAGES

*Porphyra* red algae include several kinds of seaweed called nori that are farmed in East Asia, especially Japan and China. The algae are grown on floating nets and gathered by machines. Then they are shredded and dried into thin sheets. Nori is a "sea vegetable" used in various foods and industrial processes.

Porphyra *can reproduce asexually by making two kinds of seedlike spores, monospores and aplanospores.*

*Sheets of nori can be added to noodles or flavored with spices and toasted.*

Spore grows into new thallus

Asexually produced spores

*Cultivating nori is a high-tech business.*

Cell division

Gametes fertilize

Spores float

Sexually produced carposores

Conchocelis filaments

Porphyra *sexual reproduction has several stages. The familiar large seaweed or thallus is called the sporophyte. Each of its cells has one complete set of genes, known as haploid. Cell division on the thallus produces tiny gametes (sperm and eggs), which are also haploid. The sperm and egg join to form the next stage, the gametophyte, with a double set of genes, known as diploid. The gametophyte in its carposore (container), settles on a seashell and grows into conchocelis filaments. These make their own spores, conchospores, which are haploid again. They float away and grow into new large thalli.*

Seashells such as oysters grown in beds

Conchospores released by conchocelis stage

Conchospores begin to grow into thalli

*Nori sheets are used to wrap food such as sashimi (raw seafood) and onigiri, a dish with flavored rice.*

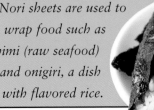

# WATER MOLDS

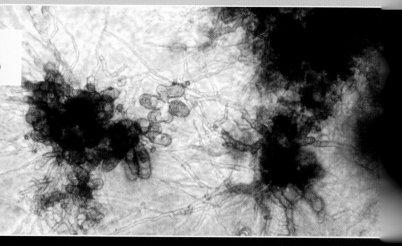

**M**ost molds are members of the Fungi kingdom. But water molds are not fungi. They are more closely related to the algal protists.

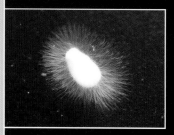

### FURRY COAT

*Water molds can grow as furry or hairy patches on plant seeds.*

### WATER-LOVERS

Water molds mostly thrive in water. They are especially common in running water, such as in rivers, in streams, around waterfalls, and in irrigation canals. They form moldlike clumps and patches of very fine hairs called mycelia, which grow over and into other living things to gain nourishment. A water mold's set of mycelia forms its main body, the thallus.

### OOSPORES

*Male and female gametes join in sexual reproduction to form hard-cased oospores.*

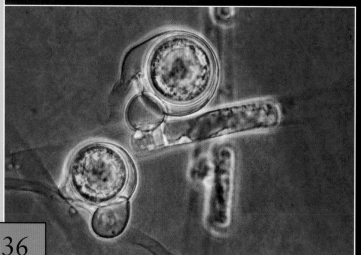

### MAKING SPORES

Pythium *water mold grows on the roots of plants, causing diseases with the same name. It produces spores (above), which are like seeds and will grow into new water molds.*

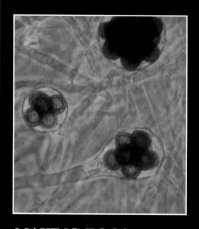

### MAKING EGGS

*The water mold's egg cells are made in capsules called oogonia.*

### COUSINS

Water molds are usually classified with protists because they do not fit into any other main group of living things, such as animals, plants, or fungi. The detailed structure of the cells that a water mold makes to move and spread, during the motile stage, shows that each cell has two flagella, one large and one small. This feature is also found in some algae, especially diatoms and brown algae. Water molds are included with diatoms and brown algae in the heterokont group.

### COTTON MOLD

*Water molds cause pale, cottonlike growths that may trap insects.*

## QUIET KILLERS

Some water molds are parasites, gaining their nutrients from other living things. Certain kinds cause serious diseases in plants and animals. Others grow on the old dead bodies of plants and animals. Like fungi, they help rot and decay. This recycles nutrients back into the soil so that new plants can grow.

## LEEK BLIGHT

*Many of the plant diseases known as blights are caused by various kinds of the water mold* Phytophthora, *a name that means "plant destroyer." White spots of the white-tip leek blight are caused by* Phytophthora porri.

## WIDESPREAD INFESTATION

*The water mold* Phytophthora cinnamomi *can destroy areas of eucalyptus or gum trees in Australia.*

## THE GREAT HUNGER

Between 1845 and 1851, a terrible disease known as late blight devastated the potato crops in Ireland. The result was the Irish potato famine. More than a million people died of hunger and illness in a few years.

## DOWNY MILDEW

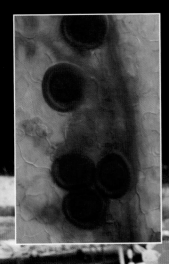

*Some diseases known as mildews are caused by water molds (left). They are common in moist greenhouses (below).*

*Irish potato blight was caused by the water mold* Phytophthora infestans *(left). Poor farmers had no food and no one to help. More than a million people left Ireland for new lives in other countries such as the U.S. and Australia. The famine is remembered by stories, songs, and works of art (right).*

The strange life-forms called slime molds are a mix of molds, amoebalike protists, mushrooms, and slugs.

## DAMP SURROUNDINGS

Slime molds are not true molds, which are fungi. But like some fungi, they form jellylike growths on trees and rotting logs, as well as in damp places among leaves, in soil, and on plants.

*HORRIBLE NAME*

*The* Fuligo septica *slime mold forms lumpy pale plasmodia. Its common name is dog's vomit mold.*

## HUNGRY HUNTERS

Some slime molds, which are also known as myceteozoans, look like blob-shaped amoebas under the microscope. They ooze along as single cells and eat bacteria, tiny fungi, and similar prey. The slime molds and their prey are taking part in the decaying process, rotting away dead plants and animals. But this amoeboid stage is only one part of the life cycle. They can form spores inside themselves, which they release to grow into new amoebas. Or they may come together for reproduction, either sexually or asexually. Their offspring then merge together and begin to grow into the next phase of the slime mold's life—a larger, jellylike blob called the plasmodium.

*WHITE JELLY*

*Slime mold plasmodia often look like lumps of pale jelly.*

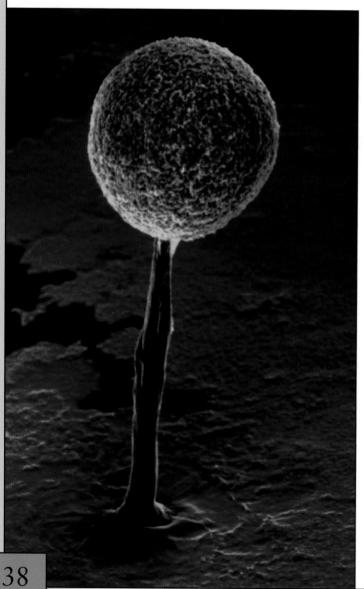

*MAKING SPORES*

*A slime mold's sporangium is usually a stalked, baglike container. Inside are tiny spores that spread by wind or water to grow into new organisms.*

## PLASMODIA

The plasmodia are the slime mold stages we usually see as slimy growths. In some species, they grow very large—some would cover a large table. They can be many colors such as yellow, pink, green, orange, or brown.

In some slime molds, the plasmodium can move by sliding along like a true amoeba. It does this by making its cytoplasm (inner fluid) flow. Over time the plasmodium forms sporangia that release spores that grow into new amoebas.

### SLIME BRAIN
Physarum polycephalum, *or "many-headed" slime, can be various shades of green or yellow. Its plasmodium feeds on bacteria and other tiny life-forms.*

### DAMP SLIME
*Several bright yellow slime molds grow in damp forests and on old wood, with nicknames such as paranvoi and witch's butter.*

### SLIMY MODELS

Some slime molds are fairly easy to keep in a laboratory or even at home. *Physarum polycephalum* is often studied by scientists to find out how it moves, feeds, and reproduces. *Physarum* survives if kept dark and damp and fed natural grains, such as oat flakes. It can be separated into lumps that grow back into larger plasmodia.

### WAVY HAIR
*Some types of slime mold plasmodia send out long "fingers" that wave slowly to look for food. Others grow upward to spread spores from their bodies into the wind.*

Dictyostelium *has a head and tail and reacts to light and water.*

# ALMOST ANIMALS

**S**ome of the strangest microscopic living things are the choanoflagellates, a name that means "collar with flagellum."

## LIKE TINY TADPOLES

Choanoflagellates are sometimes included with the protists, but some experts think they deserve their own group. Each one looks like a tiny tadpole. It has a main cell body that is egg- or ball-shaped. This head contains all the usual protist organelles, such as a nucleus with DNA, vacuoles, and energy-providing mitochondria.

## MICROVILLI

*The collar is coated with miniature sticklike parts known as microvilli. These look like bristles on a toothbrush. They make a large surface area for collecting food particles and nutrients from the water.*

Flagellum

Open end of collar

Body of collar

Base of collar

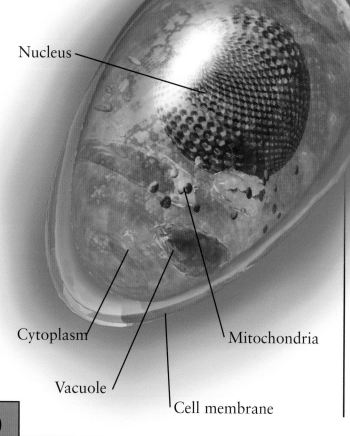

Nucleus

Cytoplasm

Mitochondria

Vacuole

Cell membrane

## CATCHING FOOD

A long flagellum sticks out of the main cell body. This twirls around to make the water-dwelling choanoflagellate swim. However, it does not move tail-first like other protists, with the flagellum at the front. Its flagellum pushes rather than pulls, so a choanoflagellate swims head-first, like a tadpole.

The collar is shaped like a funnel, with its narrow end joined to the cell body. The flagellum sticks out from its wider open end. As the flagellum twirls, it causes water to swirl around and into the collar. Tiny moving fingerlike parts called microvilli grab passing bits of food such as bacteria. They pass the food into the main cell body, where it is digested.

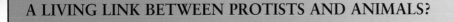

## A LIVING LINK BETWEEN PROTISTS AND ANIMALS?

*Most sponges have a hollow body with lots of tiny pores (holes) where water enters and a larger opening where it comes out.*

Choanoflagellates could be a link between single-celled living things, such as protists, and animals with lots of cells. The simplest animals are sponges. They have cells called choanocytes (collar cells), which are very similar to choanoflagellates. The choanocytes line the hollow chamber inside the sponge. Their swishing flagella draw water through the chamber, and their microvilli take in food for the whole sponge.

Exit opening

Choanocyte

Sponge body wall

Entrance pore

*The beating flagella of choanocytes force water through the sponge, allowing it to feed.*

## AROUND THE WORLD

There are more than 120 species of choanoflagellates, with more probably waiting to be discovered. They live in all kinds of water, from small ponds to the open sea and from cold, polar regions to the warm tropics. Certain species are found in all the world's oceans.

Some types of choanoflagellates group together as colonies. They stick their heads together like grapes in a bunch and attach themselves to a stalk anchored to an object, such as a rock or weed.

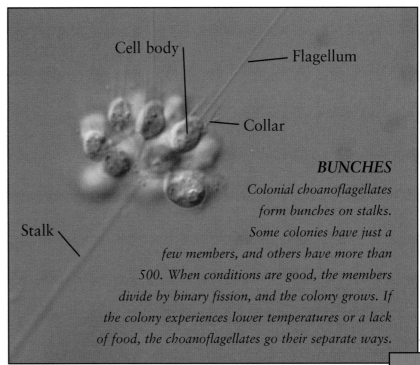

Cell body

Flagellum

Collar

Stalk

### BUNCHES

*Colonial choanoflagellates form bunches on stalks. Some colonies have just a few members, and others have more than 500. When conditions are good, the members divide by binary fission, and the colony grows. If the colony experiences lower temperatures or a lack of food, the choanoflagellates go their separate ways.*

# HARMFUL PROTISTS

**P**rotists cause some of the world's worst human diseases, killing millions of people every year. They also infest farm crops and animals, ruining harvests and making people go hungry.

## BREEDING GROUNDS

*Poor conditions, such as a lack of clean water, dirty surroundings, and open sewers, are breeding grounds for many deadly life-forms including protists.*

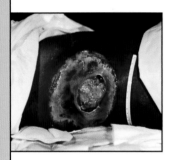

### EATEN AWAY

*Some kinds of flesh-eating amoebas do their damage in just a few hours.*

### HARMFUL AMOEBAS

Several types of amoebas enter the human body and live there as parasites. *Entamoeba histolytica* causes amoebiasis—amoebic dysentery—one of the world's most common parasitic diseases. It gets inside the body as tough-cased cysts on dirty food or fingers. It multiplies rapidly and causes severe digestive upsets and diarrhea. This tiny protist kills at least 50,000 people yearly, mainly in poor, tropical regions.

### DEADLY INVADER

*Entamoeba histolytica may stay inactive in the body without causing problems for several years.*

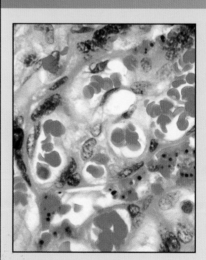

## THE SCOURGE OF MALARIA

*In a pregnant woman with malaria, the parasites may damage her placenta, which passes food and oxygen to her baby. This can harm the baby.*

Each year malaria kills more than 2 million people, most of them children. It is caused by the protist *Plasmodium*. It is spread by bites from *Anopheles* mosquitoes. Like many parasites, *Plasmodium* has a complicated life cycle involving various stages, some happening in the same host. The sporozoite stages from the mosquito first attack the body's liver, multiplying fast. They produce the next stage, the merozoites, which invade red blood cells. Malaria's main symptoms are fever, shivering, vomiting, joint pains, and convulsions.

## DIRTY WATER

*Giardia* is a protist that multiplies inside the intestines—not just of people, but of dogs, cats, cows, deer, other mammals, and some birds. Its cysts have thick walls and can survive in cold water for months, so that ponds and wells stay infested.

### CLUB-ROOT

Plasmodiophora *is the cause of club root in cabbage, cauliflower, and similar vegetables.*

## BLACK FEVER

*Certain kinds of sandflies (right) spread leishmaniasis, known as black fever. This sickness is caused by the trypanosome protist* Leishmania *(below, under the microscope). Leishmaniasis can cause skin ulcers (below). Other trypanosomes cause sleeping sickness in Africa and Chagas disease in South America.*

## TOXOPLASMOSIS

*Toxoplasma gondii* is responsible for toxoplasmosis. People catch the disease from other animals, especially cats. It produces swollen glands, aches, and pains, similar to influenza. Very rarely in children, the protists can get into the eye and damage eyesight.

### IN THE HEART

Toxoplasma *can get into heart muscle. In people already ill from other problems, it can be fatal.*

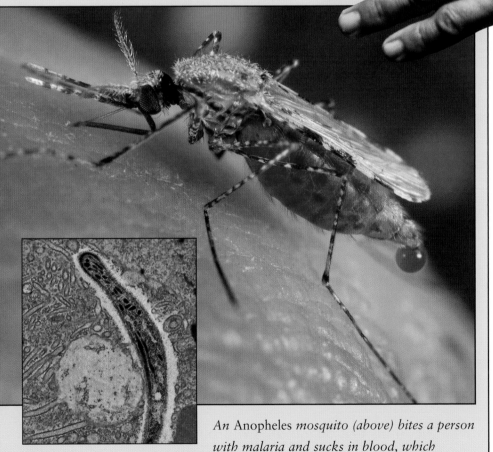

*An* Anopheles *mosquito (above) bites a person with malaria and sucks in blood, which contains* Plasmodium *protists (above left). These multiply in the mosquito and get into its saliva. Next time it bites someone with its needlelike mouth, it injects saliva to stop the blood from clotting—and also injects the protists.*

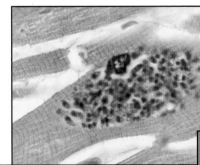

# CLASSIFICATION OF LIFE

Scientists classify living things depending on how their features and the parts inside them compare with those of other living things. In microscopic life-forms of one cell each, these parts are very tiny. But they are important, because many of them are found in the cells of much larger living things, such as plants and animals. Single-celled protists and other simple living things give us clues about how life on Earth evolved over billions of years.

The main groups of living things are known as domains. The next groups are usually kingdom, phylum (division), class, order, family, genus, and species. To see how this system works, follow the example on page 45 of how the alga *Chondrus crispus* is classified in the domain Eukarya.

## THE DOMAINS OF LIFE

### BACTERIA

 Single-celled prokaryotes, found in most places on Earth

### ARCHAEA

 Single-celled prokaryotes, many surviving in extreme conditions

### EUKARYA

#### KINGDOMS

 PROTISTA: Single-celled eukaryotes, with some simple multicelled forms

 FUNGI: Multicelled life-forms that digest their food externally

 PLANTAE: Multicelled life-forms that obtain energy by photosynthesis

 ANIMALIA: Multicelled life-forms that get their energy by taking in food

# GROUPS OF PROTISTS

Some experts classify protists with large algae or seaweeds. Others put them with plants or in their own group. They have been divided into six subkingdoms below.

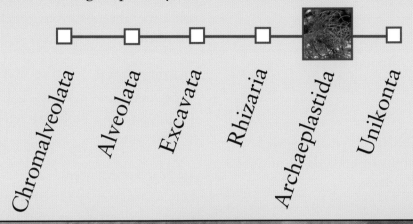

Chromalveolata Alveolata Excavata Rhizaria Archaeplastida Unikonta

*Chondrus crispus* is a red alga also known as Irish moss or carrageen. It is widely used as a food, in scientific studies, and in industry.

DOMAIN: Eukarya

SUBKINGDOM: Archaeplastida

PHYLUM: Rhodophyta

CLASS: Rhodophyceae

ORDER: Gigartinales

FAMILY: Gigartinaceae

GENUS: *Chondrus*

SPECIES: *crispus*

*Chondrus crispus* (Irish moss)

# GLOSSARY

**ASEXUAL REPRODUCTION**
Reproduction in which offspring have the same genes as the parent or parents, so they are all clones

**AUTOTROPH**
Living thing that can make its own food, usually by trapping light energy by photosynthesis

**BIOLUMINESCENCE**
Ability of living things to make light and shine or glow in the dark

**CELL MEMBRANE**
Thin covering or "skin" of a living cell such as a protist

**CHLOROPHYLL**
Green substance that captures light energy to carry out photosynthesis

**CHLOROPLAST**
Tiny part inside a cell that contains the substances needed to capture light energy and carry out photosynthesis

**CILIA**
Tiny hairlike projections from the surface of a cell that wave or beat

**CONJUGATION**
Process in which two microbes such as protists come close together and one passes DNA directly to the other

**CYST**
Small, thick-walled, tough forms of a living thing that can withstand harsh conditions

**CYTOPLASM**
Watery fluid inside a cell in which various parts float and many substances are dissolved

**DNA**
Deoxyribonucleic acid, the chemical substance that carries genetic information about how a living thing grows and survives

**EUKARYOTE**
Living cell that has an outer cell membrane and other membranes inside, enclosing parts such as the nucleus

**FLAGELLUM**
Long, bendable part of a cell that sticks out like a whip and can be be waved or twirled around for movement

**MITOCHONDRIA**
Tiny sausage-shaped parts inside a cell that break apart nutrients from food to get energy

**MYCELIA**
Tangled, threadlike network forming the main body of some living things, such as water molds and fungi

**NUCLEUS**
Control center of a living cell; contains DNA and is surrounded by a nuclear membrane

**ORGANELLE**
Main parts inside a living cell, such as the nucleus, chloroplasts, and mitochondria

**PARASITE**
Living thing that gains food, shelter, or other needs from another living thing—the host—and in the process harms the host

**PHOTOSYNTHESIS**
Capturing light energy to join simple substances and create food, which is used to grow, develop, and carry out life processes

**PLANKTON**
Millions of tiny living things floating in seas and large lakes, including many kinds of protists, as well as the eggs and young of animals

**PROKARYOTE**
Living cell that has a cell membrane covering but no other separate membranes inside, so it lacks membrane-enclosed parts, such as a nucleus

**PROTOPHYTAN**
Protist with features of a plant, such as being able to capture light energy by photosynthesis

**PROTOZOAN**
Protist with features of an animal, such as being able to move about and take in food

**PSEUDOPODS**
Armlike tentacles that some protists extend to move or capture food

**SEXUAL REPRODUCTION**
Reproduction that involves exchanging or mixing DNA, usually between the female and male, so the offspring have different genes from the parents and from each other

**SYMBIOSIS**
Relationship of two species in which both benefit from the partnership

**VACUOLE**
Pool or blob of a substance, such as water, nutrients, or waste products, inside a living cell

**Look for all the books in this series:**

*Cocci, Spirilla & Other Bacteria*
*Ferns, Mosses & Other Spore-Producing Plants*
*Molds, Mushrooms & Other Fungi*
*Protozoans, Algae & Other Protists*
*Redwoods, Hemlocks & Other*
  *Cone-Bearing Plants*
*Sunflowers, Magnolia Trees & Other*
  *Flowering Plants*

# FURTHER RESOURCES

**FURTHER READING**
Anderson, Bridget. *Come Learn With Me: The Kingdoms of Life: Classification*. New York: Lickle Publishing, 2003.

King, Katie, and Jacqueline A. Ball, eds. *Protists and Fungi*. Milwaukee: Gareth Stevens Publishing, 2004.

Pistek, Paul. *Protists and Fungi*. Logan, Iowa: Perfection Learning, 2007.

Stewart, Melissa. *Classification of Life*. Minneapolis: Twenty-First Century Books, 2008.

**INTERNET SITES**
FactHound offers a safe, fun way to find Internet sites related to this book. All of the sites on FactHound have been researched by our staff.

Here's all you do:
Visit *www.facthound.com*
FactHound will fetch the best sites for you!